THE SEARCH
TUTANKHA

JANE SHUTER

Acknowledgements

Photos

Ancient Art and Architecture Collection, page 5. Popperfoto, page 7. British Museum, page 9. Griffith Institute / Ashmolean Museum, pages 11, 13 and 17. Margaret Orr, page 18. John Frost Historical Newspaper Service, page 20.

Illustrations

Angus McBride (Linden Artists), page 16 middle. Denis Ryan, page 21 (illustrations on 'Goosebumps' books covers – reproduced by kind permission of Scholastic Ltd). All other illustrations by Roger Stewart and Nick Harris.

Heinemann Educational Publishers
Halley Court, Jordan Hill, Oxford OX2 8EJ
a division of Reed Educational & Professional Publishing Limited
www.heinemann.co.uk

Heinemann is a registered trademark of Reed Educational & Professional Publishing Limited

First published 2000
Original edition © Jane Shuter 1998
Literacy World Satellites edition © Jane Shuter 2000
Additional writing for Satellites edition by Wendy Cobb

04 03 02 01 00
10 9 8 7 6 5 4 3 2 1

ISBN 0 435 11891 9   *LW Satellites: The Search for Tutankhamen* single copy

ISBN 0 435 11895 1   *LW Satellites: The Search for Tutankhamen* 6 copy pack

Designed by M2
Printed and bound in the UK

Also available at Stage 1 of *Literacy World Satellites*

ISBN 0 435 11893 5   *LW Satellites: Incredible Insects* single copy
ISBN 0 435 11897 8   *LW Satellites: Incredible Insects* 6 copy pack

ISBN 0 435 11892 7   *LW Satellites: Making the Past into Presents* single copy
ISBN 0 435 11896 X   *LW Satellites: Making the Past into Presents* 6 copy pack

ISBN 0 435 11894 3   *LW Satellites: How a Book is Made* single copy
ISBN 0 435 11898 6   *LW Satellites: How a Book is Made* 6 copy pack

ISBN 0 435 11900 1   *LW Satellites: Teacher's Guide Stage 1*
ISBN 0 435 11899 4   *LW Satellites: Guided Reading Cards Stage 1*

CONTENTS

INTRODUCTION

Mediterranean Sea

The Delta

EGYPT

Cairo

River Nile

The Valley of
the Kings

Thebes

SECRET TOMBS

This book is about the hunt for
the **tomb** of Tutankhamen. He
was king of **Egypt** about 3,000
years ago.

When kings of Egypt died, they
were buried in tombs. These
tombs were cut deep into rocks
in the **Valley of the Kings**.

TREASURE

The tombs were filled with the
kings' treasure. There was gold,
silver and jewels. People spent
many years trying to find the
tombs and the treasure.

Scale

| 0 | 125km | 250km | 375km | 500km |

1cm on the map = 125km on the ground

Most of Egypt was
desert, so the people
lived near the river.

SEARCHING FOR TREASURE

Hundreds of years passed, but people did not forget about the treasure. Soldiers guarded the tombs. Anyone caught stealing was killed.

As more time passed, sand blew over the tombs. It was hard to find the doorways to the tombs but people carried on looking for the buried treasure.

This photo shows how hard it was to know where to start digging.

The Valley of the Kings, where many kings were buried.

THE MISSING KING

TUTANKHAMEN'S TOMB

Archaeologists knew that Tutankhamen's tomb was somewhere in the Valley of the Kings. But they thought they would never find it.

STOLEN?

Even if the tomb was found, they were sure all the treasure would have been stolen many years before.

The mummy case that held Tutankhamen's body. It is made of gold and jewels.

TIMELINE

1890	1895	1900	1905

1891 Howard Carter first went to work in Egypt, aged 17

1899 – 1905 Carter helped to excavate the Valley of the Kings

1907 Lord Carnarvon went to Egypt and met Carter

THE ARCHAEOLOGISTS

Howard Carter was an archaeologist. He was sure that he could find Tutankhamen's tomb.

Lord Carnarvon collected treasures from Egypt. He wanted to help find the tomb. Because he was rich he could pay for the search.

The two men worked together to **excavate** the Valley of the Kings from 1914 to 1923.

Howard Carter

Lord Carnarvon

1910   1915   1920   1925

1914 – 1923 Carter and Carnarvon excavated
the Valley of the Kings

7

PERMISSION TO DIG

WAITING

Only one team of archaeologists at a time was allowed to dig in the Valley of the Kings. A team was already digging there in 1907, so Carter went to Thebes instead. He worked there until 1912.

DIGGING IN THE DELTA

In 1913 Carter tried digging in the Delta. This is the land where the River Nile meets the sea. But first the dig was flooded, then it was over-run by cobras.

Thebes and the Delta are on the map on page 4.

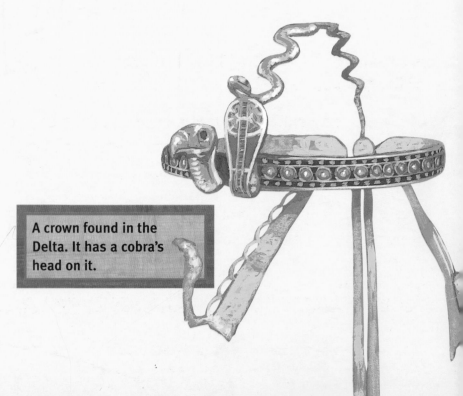

A crown found in the Delta. It has a cobra's head on it.

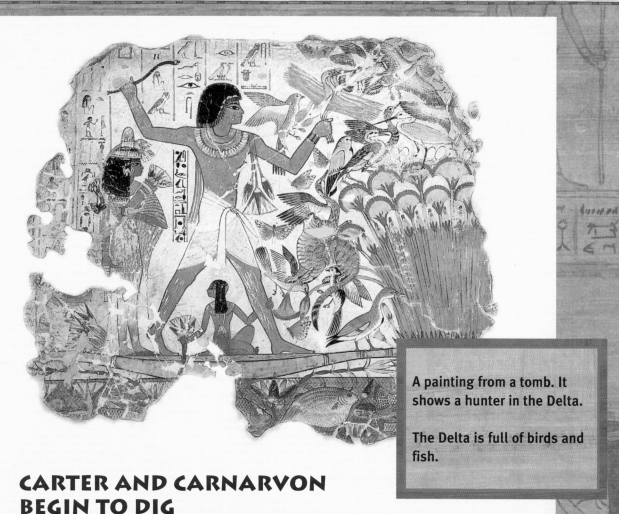

A painting from a tomb. It shows a hunter in the Delta.

The Delta is full of birds and fish.

CARTER AND CARNARVON BEGIN TO DIG

In 1914, Carter and Carnarvon finally had a chance to dig in the Valley of the Kings. But, just as they started, the **First World War** began.

There was fighting in Egypt during the war. This meant that they couldn't dig in the Valley of the Kings for three more years.

1910   1915   1920   1925

1914 Carnarvon and Carter got permission to excavate the Valley of the Kings

1917 Excavation began

SLOW BEGINNINGS

CARTER'S PLAN

Carter told the workers to dig through the sand until they got down to hard rock. It was very slow work.

SIX HARD YEARS

Six years passed, but Carter had still not found the tomb. Lord Carnarvon felt that he had paid lots of money for the dig, but nothing had been found. So he told Carter to come back to England.

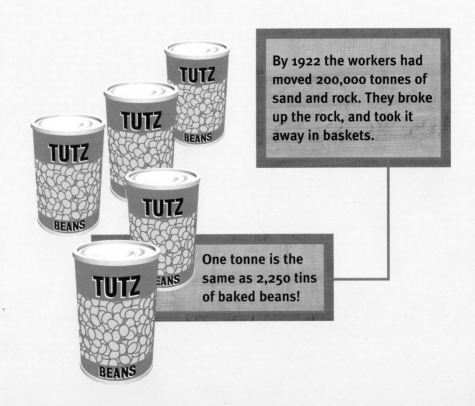

By 1922 the workers had moved 200,000 tonnes of sand and rock. They broke up the rock, and took it away in baskets.

One tonne is the same as 2,250 tins of baked beans!

ONE LAST CHANCE

Lord Carnarvon told Carter that he could not have any more
money. This was in the summer of 1922. Carter begged him for
just one more year. He said he would pay the money back if he
did not find the tomb. Lord Carnarvon agreed.

1910	1915	1920	1925

1917–1922 Carter found
nothing

Summer 1922 Carter begged
Carnarvon for one more year

THE RIGHT TOMB?

CARTER FINDS A TOMB

Carter started digging again on 1 November 1922. The workers soon found some steps and a door with Tutankhamen's name on it. But Carter could tell that the door had been opened, long ago. Had the treasure already been stolen?

They were all very excited, but Carter had promised to wait for Lord Carnarvon to get there before they opened the door.

AT LAST!

Lord Carnarvon arrived on 24 November. Two days later, they found another door. Carter took out some bricks. He lit a candle and looked through the hole. There was a long silence.

At last, Lord Carnarvon asked Carter if he could see anything. Carter said, 'Yes, wonderful things.'

6 November
Door found

26 November Door to the antechamber opened

November 1922 · 1 2 3 4 5 6 7 8 9 10 11 12 13 14 15 16 17 18 19 20 21 22 23 24 25 26 27 28 29 30

4 November
First step found

24 November
Lord Carnarvon arrived

When Carter looked inside the tomb, he saw gold everywhere.

A drawing of the gold bed Carter saw in the tomb.

1910   1915   1920   1925

1922

TUTANKHAMEN FOUND

THE ANTECHAMBER

The first room Carter went into was the antechamber.
He could see it had been robbed.

Carter could see the door to the burial chamber.
It was guarded by two statues.
This room had been broken into as well.

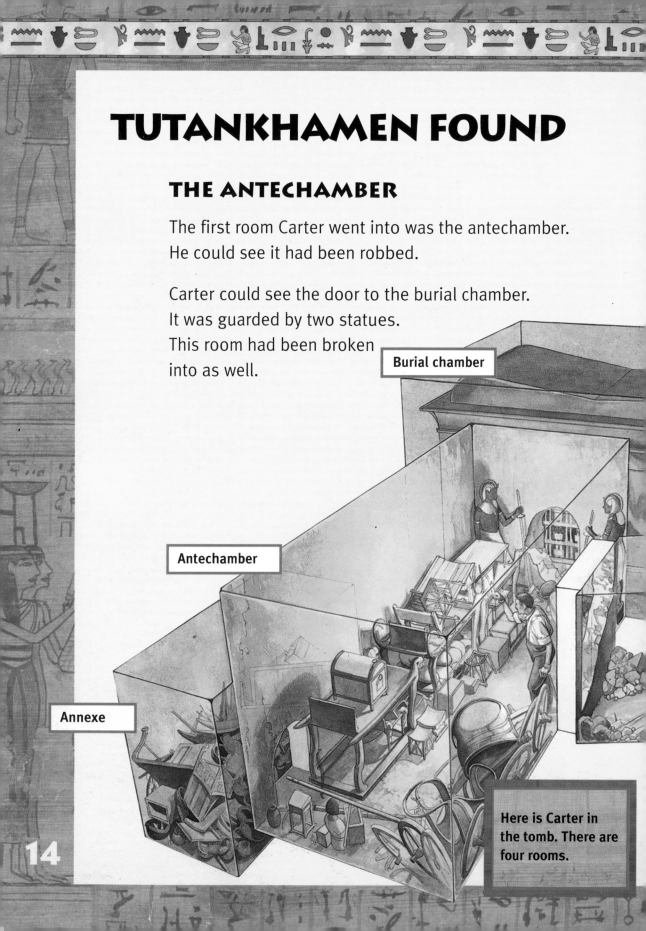

Burial chamber

Antechamber

Annexe

Here is Carter in the tomb. There are four rooms.

THE DEAD KING

On 17 February 1923 the workers opened the burial chamber. Tutankhamen's body was still there! The body was inside:

- three mummy cases
- one stone box
- four golden **shrines.**

TREASURE

All four rooms were full of treasure. Carter was scared it would all be stolen. So the archaeologists started to move it to a safe place. It took years to clear it all out.

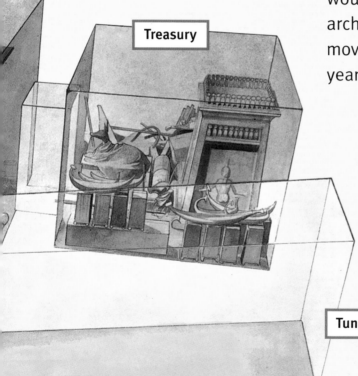

Treasury

Tunnel

1910   1915   1920   1925

December 1922 – February 1923
Treasures in the antechamber
sorted, packed and moved to safety

17 February 1923
Door to the burial
chamber opened

UNPACKING THE MUMMY

OPENING THE CASES

1st shrine

2nd shrine

3rd shrine

4th shrine

Stone box

It took more than two years to unpack Tutankhamen's **mummy.** First the archaeologists took off the four gold shrines. Then they opened the stone box. Next they opened the three mummy cases. Finally they found the king's mummy.

1st mummy case

2nd mummy case

The golden death mask on the mummy weighed 10.25 kg.

3rd mummy case

10 October 1925 They started to open the mummy cases

November 1927 They started taking the treasure from the last room

| 1923 | 1924 | 1925 | 1926 | 1927 |

March 1923 The archaeologists started to take off the shrines

28 October 1925 They reached the mummy

The unwrapped mummy
of Tutankhamen.

UNWRAPPING THE MUMMY

At last the archaeologists started to unwrap the mummy. It was wrapped in strips of cloth. If the strips were laid out end to end, they would be nearly 1000 metres long!

But the mummy was damaged. Many bones were broken.

WHY WAS IT DAMAGED?

No-one knows how the mummy got damaged. They tried to be very careful when they unwrapped it. Some people think it was not **embalmed** properly.

1910　1915　1920　1925

PROBLEMS

VISITORS

Lots of people wanted to see the tomb of Tutankhamen. Many important people came from all over the world. This made it very hard to get on with the work.

A chair found in the tomb.

Some of the visitors having lunch in a nearby tomb. Howard Carter is on the right, in the middle.

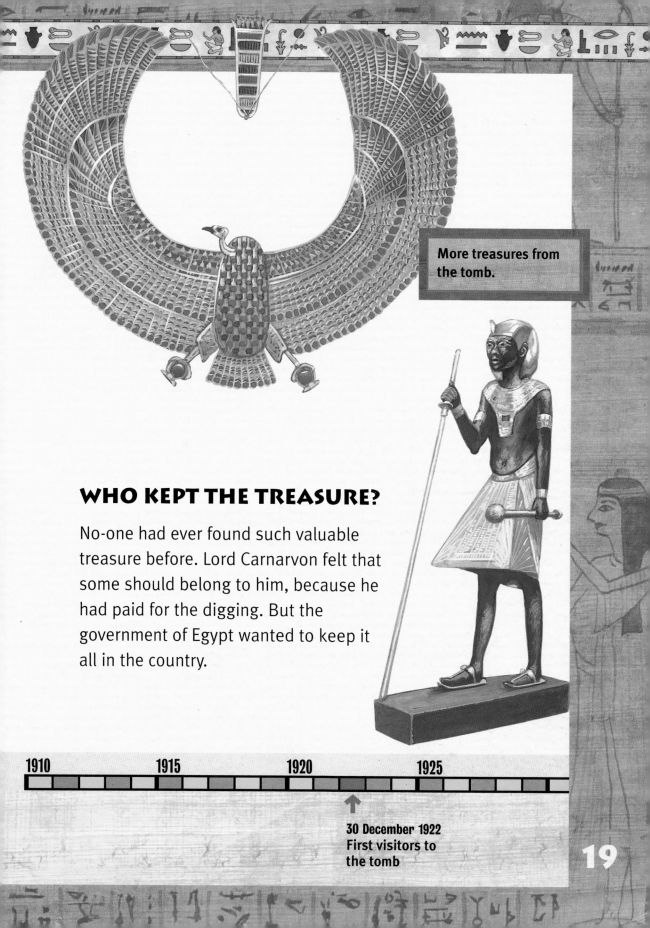

More treasures from the tomb.

WHO KEPT THE TREASURE?

No-one had ever found such valuable treasure before. Lord Carnarvon felt that some should belong to him, because he had paid for the digging. But the government of Egypt wanted to keep it all in the country.

1910   1915   1920   1925

↑
30 December 1922
First visitors to
the tomb

CURSED!

LORD CARNARVON'S DEATH

Lord Carnarvon died in Cairo in 1923. As he died, two strange things happened. In Cairo all the lights went out, and back in England his dog howled and died.

THE CURSE

The newspapers said his death was the revenge of Tutankhamen. By 1924 some more people who worked on the tomb had also died. The story of the curse grew stronger.

Exploding Tutankhamen 'Curse' Myth

ALL ALIVE WHO SAW UNWRAPPING OF MUMMY

From Our Own Correspondent
NEW YORK, Friday.
Strenuous efforts to lay the ghost of Tutankhamen and to

"CURSE" OF THE PHARAOHS.

TEN DEATHS OF TUT TOMB PARTY.

The ancient curse of the Egyptians— "Death shall come on swift wings to him that toucheth the tomb of a Pharaoh "—was quoted once again yesterday when news reached England that a tenth person connected with the discovery of the tomb of Tutankhamen had met a tragic fate in the United States.

He was Dr. Jonathan W. H. Carver, who was killed in a motor smash at Columbus, Texas. His assistant, Mr. H. H. Miller, who was slightly injured.

TUTANKHAMEN'S CURSE AGAIN?

SCIENTISTS AND QUEER ACCIDENTS

From Our Special Correspondent
OXFORD, Friday.
"**D**EATH shall come on swift wings to him that toucheth the tomb of Pharaoh."
Once more the baneful influence of this curse of Ancient Egypt is

Curse Disproved
AMONG those who did most to disprove the belief that the

DEATH OF MR. H. CARTER

MAN WHO FOUND TOMB OF TUTANKHAMEN

"NEVER BELIEVED IN CURSE"

Mr. Howard Carter who, with the late Earl of Carnarvon, discovered the tomb of King

Some newspaper headlines.

JUST A GOOD STORY?

None of the workers believed the curse. Carter and the man who unwrapped the mummy lived on. If Tutankhamen wanted revenge, these are the people who would have died first.

It was a good story and many books and films have used it to scare us.

These books use the idea of the mummy's curse.

1910   1915   1920   1925

5 April 1923 Lord Carnarvon died in Cairo

TIMELINE

1891 Howard Carter went to work in Egypt, aged 17

1899 – 1905 Carter helped to dig in the Valley of the Kings

1907 Lord Carnarvon went to Egypt and met Carter

1914 Carnarvon and Carter got permission to excavate the Valley of the Kings

1917 Excavation began

1917 – 1922 Carter found nothing

1922 summer Carter begged for one more year

December 1922 – February 1923 Treasures in the antechamber sorted, packed and moved to safety

November 1927 Treasure taken from the last room

1922
4 November First step found

6 November Outer door found

24 November Carnarvon arrived in Egypt

26 November Door to the antechamber found and opened

30 December First visitors to the tomb

1925
10 October Archaeologists started to open the mummy cases

28 October They reached the mummy

1890
1891
1892
1893
1894
1895
1896
1897
1898
1899
1900
1901
1902
1903
1904
1905
1906
1907
1908
1909
1910
1911
1912
1913
1914
1915
1916
1917
1918
1919
1920
1921
1922
1923
1924
1925
1926
1927
1928
1929

GLOSSARY

archaeologist
a person who excavates places people have used in the past

Cairo
the most important city in Egypt

death mask
a mask put over the face of a mummy, painted to look like the dead person

the Delta
the marshy part of Egypt where the River Nile runs into the sea

Egypt
a country on the coast of Africa

to embalm
to soak a body in oils and wrap it in strips of cloth so that it does not rot

excavate
to clear away layers of soil very carefully

First World War
a war that lasted from 1914 to 1918

mummy
the embalmed body of a dead person or animal

mummy case
the painted case that a mummy was buried in

shrine
a box or container, covered in holy pictures

Thebes
a city in Egypt

tomb
a place where a dead person is buried

Valley of the Kings
the place where the Egyptians buried their kings

INDEX